In whatever area of life one may meet the challenge of courage, whatever might be the sacrifices he faces if he follows his conscience ... each man must decide for himself the course he will follow. The stories of past courage can define that ingredient - they can teach, they can offer hope, they can provide inspiration. But they cannot supply courage itself. For this each man must look into his own soul.

John F. Kennedy

Mere Existentialism: A Primer

Max Malikow

Mere Existentialism: A Primer

Published by: Theocentric Publishing Group
                 1069 Main Street
                 Chipley, Florida 32428
                 http://www.theocentricpublishing.com

Library of Congress Control Number: 2014946518

ISBN 9780991481132

To Louis Malikow: Whose decency and integrity has provided an excellent example for a younger brother.

To S.C. Who has lived out these words better than anyone I have ever known: "let us not love with words or tongue but with actions and in truth" (1 John 3:18).

Acknowledgments

Everything begins somewhere. The idea for this primer began when Le Moyne College Philosophy Department Chair Mario Saenz asked me to teach the course, *Existentialism: Gabriel Marcel.* I was encouraged by his confidence in me and pleased to accept the assignment. As is always the case, to teach is to learn. Teaching existentialism not only added to my repertoire of courses but expanded my thinking about life in general and my own life in particular. The publication of this little book provides an occasion to acknowledge Professor Saenz's unwitting contribution to my development as a teacher and person. Also deserving of recognition is Diane Coville for her artistic contribution to this project.

Preface

William of Ockham, a 14th century Franciscan friar, articulated a guiding principle for efficient reasoning that bears his name: Ockham's Razor. Also known as the *principle of parsimony*, it teaches that explanations should be as uncomplicated as possible. Its Latin expression is, *Entia non sunt multiplicanda praeter necessitatem*. Translated into English, it reads, "Entities should not be multiplied beyond necessity."

This book is a *primer*, which is to say it is a small introductory book intended to provide a rudimentary understanding of existentialism. Its title includes the word *mere*, which implies it is written in the spirit of *Ockham's Razor*. Anyone who is familiar with existentialism and searching for advanced knowledge of the subject would be better served to seek out another book.

The introduction consists of brief answers to five questions:

1. What is existentialism?
2. Why is it called existentialism?
3. When did existentialism begin?
4. What ideas do existentialists have in common?
5. What are some recurring existential themes?

Each of the nine chapters describes at least one significant contribution made by the philosopher or writer featured in that chapter. (They appear in the chronological order of their birth.) The epilogue consists of nine questions, one from each of the existentialists presented in this primer. It provides an opportunity for review and introspection. The book concludes with a glossary of accumulated technical terms.

Finally, this book is written in the first person voice, giving it a relaxed quality. Its vernacular style is intended to make it as "user friendly" as possible. The first person is apropo for this work given its subject. Existentialism is, "the philosophical method that studies human existence from inside the subject's experience rather than from outside. It takes a first person or subjective approach to the ultimate questions rather than a third person or objective approach" (Pojman, 1991, 631).

Max Malikow
Syracuse, NY
May 7, 2014

Table of Contents

Introduction

What is existentialism?

Existentialism is a philosophical movement, mostly associated with the 20th century, concerned with an individual's existence in an unfathomable universe. Further, existentialism views the human condition as an unfortunate situation in which we must assume full responsibility for our actions without any certain knowledge of what is right or wrong or good or bad. The late Professor Robert Solomon of the University of Texas at Austin named his existentialism course: "No Excuses: Existentialism and the Meaning of Life." He introduced his course with this description:

> The message of existentialism ... is about as simple as can be. It is that every one of us, as an individual, is responsible - responsible for what we do, responsible for who we are, responsible for the way we face and deal with the world, responsible, ultimately, for the way the world is. It is, in a very short phrase, the philosophy of "no excuses!" (2000, 1).

Why is it called existentialism?

It is called existentialism because it is the philosophical study of existence - specifically, human existence. Unlike objects, like apples and zucchinis, or animals, like aardvarks and zebras, human beings are aware of their existence. Therein lies the problem. With self-awareness comes a myriad of issues, not the least of which is *the meaning of life.* Expressed as a question, this issue is: *What actions do I need to bring into existence in order to bring meaning to my life?*

An anecdote (perhaps a myth) associated with the legendary college basketball coach Bobby Knight provides a spot-on characterization of existentialism. Annually, at the first practice for the coming season, he would tell his players they have great potential. Coach Knight then would proceed to tell them his definition of potential: "You haven't done anything yet." The same thought was expressed by the renown psychiatrist Thomas Szasz when he wrote wrote: "People often say that this or that person has not yet found himself. But the self is not something one finds, it is something one creates" (1973, 49). Like Knight, he believed we create ourselves by our actions.

When did existentialism begin?

Who was the first existentialist? To answer that question, we would have to know the first person to wonder if his life was worth living or the first person to feel the burden of responsibility for the consequences that emanated from her actions.

Existential thoughts are embedded in the teaching of Jesus, who told his disciples, "If you love me, you will *keep* my commandments" (John 14:15, NIV). He challenged a wealthy young man to *sell* his possessions, *distribute* the proceeds to the poor, and *follow* as a disciple (Luke 18:18-27). (The verbs are italicized to emphasize action.)

The philosophy that preceded existentialism and contributed to it is *phenomenology*, a system of thought associated with Edmund Husserl (1859-1938). Martin Heidegger, who is featured in chapter

IV, was a student of Husserl. Phenomenology is the belief that an individual's conscious experience of the world is more important, psychologically, than the real world itself. In other words, a reality broader than our experience might exist, but it is only our experience of reality that matters to us. The reason for this is captured by an aphorism: *We do not see things as they are; we see them as we are*. Stated in even fewer words: perception is reality.

If the origin of existentialism is traced to its earliest formal expression, it would be the writings of two nineteenth century philosophers, Soren Kierkegaard and Friedrich Nietzsche. Ironically, Nietzsche was as passionate an atheist as Kierkegaard was a Christian. Nevertheless, each thought the religious and philosophical thinking of his day provided inadequate answers to the fundamental questions of life. Shakespeare wrote, "The poet gives to airy abstraction a local habitation and a name" (*A Midsummer Night's Dream*, Act V, scene 1). Kierkegaard and Nietzsche believed religion and philosophy up to the nineteenth century offered airy abstractions that were ethereal and impractical. They believed life is something to be lived, not merely contemplated. They agreed with Albert Camus, who came after them and wrote: "You will never live if you're looking for the meaning of life" (2014).

What ideas do existentialists have in common?

As diverse as the existentialist writers are, they agree on at least four basic principles. First, there is no such thing as *human nature*, therefore no one is compelled to act in a predetermined manner. And since there are no standardized human beings, we are individually responsible for our actions. The author and psychiatrist Scott Peck emphasized this when he wrote:

> Triggers are pulled by individuals. Orders are given and executed by individuals. In the last analysis, every single human act is ultimately the result of an individual choice (1983, 215).

Second, life cannot be managed by any set of rules. Real life includes situations that call for exceptions to any rule, even the ones considered sacrosanct. For example, although we have been taught to tell the truth always, there will be occasions when lying will be the wiser or kinder thing to do.

Third, just as nutritionists tell us, "You are what you eat," existentialists insist, "You are what you do." As the eminent psychiatrist Carl Jung said, "You are what you do, not what you say you'll do" (2014).

Fourth, we experience life as we actually are, not as we imagine ourselves to be. In a disagreement it's not unusual for one person to say to another, "If you were me, how would you feel?" The fact is, no matter how empathic we might be, we cannot experience the feelings of another person.

What are some recurring existential themes?

In addition to these four basic principles, existential literature has at least ten recurring themes. Although not addressed by every writer, they are present often enough to justify our attention.

1. **Absurdity**: There is no meaning to life except the meaning each of us determines for himself. Shakespeare's Macbeth was nearly right when he assessed life as "full of sound and fury, signifying nothing" (*Macbeth*, Act V, scene 5). Our lives *can* be significant if we determine to make them so. In addition, absurdity is the conflict between our rational expectations of the world (justice, satisfaction, happiness) and the world's callous indifference to our expectations.

2. **Alienation**: To a degree, we are strangers to ourselves; beings who are deficient in self-understanding. Like Robert Ludlow's fictional character, Jason Bourne, we are trying to extrapolate who we are from our thoughts and actions.

3. **Anxiety**: Also referred to as *existential angst*, it is the inner turmoil we experience when we come to the realization that life has no meaning.

4. **Authenticity**: For each of us, our true self is determined by our actions. Jean-Paul Sartre believed we are engaged in self-deception when we think we are defined by our intentions. Moreover, we have the tendency to deceive ourselves about why we do what we do, thereby compounding the error. Sartre referred to such self-deception as *bad faith*.

5. **Death**: Simply stated, the impermanence of all we do makes life meaningless. A popular 1970's song, "Dust in the Wind," combines the themes of absurdity, anxiety, self-deception, and death in a single line: "All we do, crumbles to the ground though we refuse to see" (Livgren, 1977).

6. **Forlornness**: The feeling that comes upon us when we realize no one can help us make sense of our existence. Like a prisoner of war held in solitary confinement, we are on our own to determine what we need to do if our existence is to have meaning.

7. **Individuality**: There is no philosophy, religion, science or any other system of thought that can provide us with the meaning of life. There is no "suit off the rack;" there is no "one-size-fits-all." All suits are "tailor made" by the wearer. Delivering a commencement address at Stanford University, the late Steve Jobs said, "To live according to dogma is to live according to someone else's thinking" (2005).

8. **Passionate Engagement**: Not everyone has the same interests. One of life's challenges is to discover the activities that truly matter to us and pursue them. This discovery is essential to an authentic life. For Viktor Frankl, virtually everyday, life provides innumerable opportunities for meaningful, passionate engagement.

9. **Rejection of Meaning-Giving Narratives**: There is no story from literature, fiction or nonfiction, that can provide us with the purpose of our life. The French essayist and playwright Gabriel Marcel (1889-1973) inquired into the meaning of life by arousing the dramatic imagination. But he even agreed with Camus that we bear the weight of our own existence.

10. **Responsibility**: Jean-Paul Sartre wrote: "Man is condemned to be free, condemned because he did not create himself, yet, nonetheless free, because once cast into the world he is responsible for

everything he does" (1957, 23). He believed we cannot unburden ourselves of this responsibility by protesting, "I didn't ask to be born!"

"Margaret," a film written and directed by Kenneth Lonergan, incorporates several of existentialism's recurring themes (2011). In the movie, a seventeen year-old girl, Lisa Cohen, distracts a bus driver who runs a red light and strikes a woman, killing her. In a powerful, emotionally provocative scene the woman dies in Lisa's arms. The existential themes raised in this scene are:

1. Life can end suddenly, doing something as ordinary as crossing a street. (absurdity, death)

2. Lisa realizes what happened to the woman can happen to anyone, including Lisa herself. (anxiety)

3. Three people stepped forward to help the dying woman; they took action in a tragic situation. (authenticity)

4. Lisa provided a measure of comfort, but not meaning, for the dying woman. (forlornness)

5. Both Lisa and the bus driver are responsible for this accident. (responsibility)

6. Lisa and the two men who came forward to help are doing their best in a hopeless situation. (passionate engagement)

7. The dying woman asks that her daughter be contacted. (death)

8. This scene cannot provide us with a meaning for our lives. Our lives are too diverse to derive one meaning for all of us. However, it can have an influence on some aspect of our life if we make the application. (rejection of meaning-giving narratives)

I.   Soren Kierkegaard (1813-1855): *A Leap to Faith*

Kierkegaard's philosophy was existentialist in the deepest sense, for he understood completely that man must get beyond the artificialities of life. This means he must not take the easy way out by following forms and rituals.

- Thomas Ellis Katen

If you are talking to God, you are praying. But if God talks to you, you have schizophrenia.

- Thomas Szasz

Ironically, the phrase most often associated with Soren Kierkegaard is one that is frequently misunderstood. Nowhere in his writings did he advocate a "leap *of* faith." Instead, he favored a "leap *to* faith." A leap *to* faith is acting decisively in situations of uncertain outcome. It is a leap beyond knowledge and reason, which he viewed as limited and insufficient for life management. Kierkegaard asked, "What then is the Unknown?" He answered, "It is the limit to which Reason repeatedly comes" (2014).

A prolific writer, in his forty-two year life he produced 18,000 pages of journal entries and thirty published works. In one of his most influential works, *Fear and Trembling*, he presents the biblical patriarch Abraham as the paradigm of authentic faith and an example of religion in its most profound expression (1843). Abraham was obedient to God's directive to sacrifice Isaac.

Some time later God tested Abraham. He said to him, "Abraham!" "Here I am," he replied. Then God said, "Take your son, your only son, Isaac, whom you love, and go to the region of Moriah. Sacrifice him there as a burnt offering

on one of the mountains I will tell you about." (Genesis
22:1,2)

God called Abraham to do something humanly incompre-
hensible, thereby creating a paradox beyond reason's capacity for
resolution. Subsequently, God sent an angelic messenger to rescind
the mandate, but not before Abraham had prepared an altar and
taken knife in hand.

> "Do not lay a hand on the boy," (God) said. "Do not do
> anything to him. Now I know that you fear God, because
> you have not withheld from me your son, your only son"
> (Genesis 22:12).

The Abraham story has a dramatic counterpart in the movie,
"Field of Dreams," adapted from W.P. Kinsella's novel, *Shoeless Joe*
(1982). In both versions, an Iowa farmer, Ray Kinsella, hears a voice
when working in his corn field. The voice instructs him to plow his
crop under and build a baseball field where the corn was growing.
(This is the occasion for the well-known quotation: "If you build it
he will come.") With his jeering neighbors looking on in disbelief,
Ray plows the corn under and builds the baseball field. Like
Abraham, Ray was obedient to the inner calling to act in defiance of
reason and common sense.

Dietrich Bonhoeffer's paradox is a real-life instance of a
man of faith confronted with conflicting convictions. A prominent
Lutheran pastor, theologian, and anti-Nazi dissident in Germany
during World War II, he participated in a plot to assassinate Adolf
Hitler. After the plot failed Bonhoeffer was convicted of treason
and executed in a concentration camp. His paradox was the
contradiction between his conviction that he needed to do

something more than preach and write in opposition to the Nazi regime and the biblical commandment, "Thou shalt not kill" (Exodus 20:13). Presciently, eight years before his death, Bonhoeffer wrote, "When Christ calls a man, he bids him come and die" (1995, 88).

Alluded to in the Introduction is Jesus' challenge to the Rich Ruler, narrated in the *New Testament*: "Sell everything you have and give to the poor, and you will have treasure in heaven. Then come follow me" (Luke 18:22). The Rich Ruler drew back from this calling, prompting Jesus to say, "How hard it is for the rich to enter the kingdom of God. Indeed, it is easier for a camel to go through the eye of a needle than for a rich man to enter the kingdom of God" (Luke 18:24,25). Indeed, it is counterintuitive to abandon great wealth and the comfort it provides in order to walk an uncertain path.

Any consideration of Kierkegaard's concept of a leap *to* faith must include the auditory hallucinations experienced by some psychotic patients. In 2001 a Dallas, Texas mother, Andrea Yates, drowned her five children in a bathtub. (Four boys and a girl, ranging in age from seven years to six months.) Yates claimed that for over two years she had been resisting a voice telling her she was an evil woman raising evil children, who needed to die. The psychiatric testimony given at her trial included a diagnosis of postpartum psychosis. Currently she is residing in a prison psychiatric hospital.

Kierkegaard's Three Modes of Existence

Several of Kierkegaard's books were written under pseudonyms. He believed writing under names other than his own would assist his readers in reaching their own conclusions, undistracted by any influence he might have had on them. Two of these works include his notion of *three modes of existence*. Expounding more like a developmental psychologist than a philosopher, Kierkegaard asserted human beings move through three stages en route to the true or authentic self. In *Either/Or* (Victor Eremita, 1972) and *Stages on Life's Way* (Hilarious Bookbinder, 1972) he described the *aesthetic, ethical*, and *religious modes of existence*.

The word aesthetic is derived from the Greek *aisthetikos* - pertaining to the senses. Kierkegaard characterized the first stage of life as devoted to experiencing pleasure and avoiding pain. Similar to Hedonism, an ancient Greek philosophy, individuals living in the *aesthetic mode of existence* contemplate their activities by calculating the pleasure and/or pain to be derived from a given action. An example of an individual who lived in this mode is Otto Gross, a psychiatrist and contemporary of Sigmund Freud and Carl Jung, both of whom treated Gross as a patient in psychoanalysis. Dr. Gross believed there should be no suppression of the sexual drive owing to its power and the pleasure to be gleaned from not restraining it.

At the other extreme is T.S. Eliot's poetic character J. Alfred Prufrock. In the poem that bears his name, Prufrock's fear of the pain of rejection precludes him from declaring his love for the woman he desires (1915). After weighing the possibility of joy against the prospect of rejection, he decided not to declare his romantic interest. Sadly, the poem ends with Prufrock living out his years alone.

The *ethical mode of existence* is characterized by a life guided by an internalized code of conduct. Aristotle's formulaic definition of happiness (Greek *eudaimonia*) requires life to be lived in accordance with highest virtue. In Aaron Sorkin's play, *A Few Good Men*, a Marine corporal named Harold Dawson affirms the code by which he and other Marines live: *unit, Corps, God, country* (1989). However, even an unwavering commitment to a moral code can be questionable. When Jesus healed a woman on the Sabbath, one of his adversaries indicted him for breaking one of the Ten Commandments. Jesus used the occasion to explain that inflexible adherence to the law is unconscionable when it is detrimental to life. He communicated the same idea on another occasion when he said, "The Sabbath was made for man, not man for the Sabbath (Mark 2:27).

The flexibility of which Jesus spoke is compatible with Kierkegaard's *religious mode of existence.*

> The leap from the ethical to the religious happens when one encounters a situation which goes beyond ethical rules ... When one must break with the rules that are accepted in the society in which one lives in order to achieve something that may go beyond the norm, but which is true to one's inner calling, he has entered the level of life Kierkegaard calls the religious (Cogswell, 2008, 54).

Recall the words of Steve Jobs given in the Introduction: "To live according to dogma is to live according to someone else's thinking" (2005). Existentialists believe religious dogma deauthenticates people when they follow rules and traditions without thinking. Kierkegaard, a Christian existentialist, insisted one of the great challenges of religious life is determining when to break the rules and deviate from tradition. Had he known Bonhoeffer, Kierkegaard likely would have offered him alongside Abraham as an example of the *religious mode of existence.*

II. Friedrich Nietzsche (1844-1900): *The Death of God*

Of all that is written, I care only for what is written in blood.

                                          - Friedrich Nietzsche

Jesus Christ taught about eternal life and the Kingdom of God. Karl Marx wrote of a future proletarian revolution and resultant classless society. In contrast to Jesus and Marx, Friedrich Nietzsche eschewed "other-worldly" thinking. For him, *this* life is the only one that is certain because it is present in the present.

There are several reasons for categorizing Nietzsche as an existentialist. Existentialists believe determinism is the hand we've been dealt and free will is how we choose to play that hand. Nietzsche was dealt a bad hand in terms of physical health yet wrote, "That which does not kill me makes me stronger" (2014).

Recurring in Nietzsche's writing is a Latin phrase, *amor fati* (love your fate). He believed since we did not choose the time and place of our birth as well as many other features of our life, fate has placed us in an unchosen context. Nevertheless, we are responsible for exercising free will and creating the fate we can love.

Nietzsche was an immoralist, which is not to say he was an evildoer. Rather, it means he challenged the established morality of his day. According to him we do not realize our own morality by blind conformity to a pre-existing code of conduct, like the Ten Commandments or Sermon on the Mount. Instead, we declare our morality by our actions. This credo is consistent with Nietzsche's atheism, which he addressed in his last book, *Ecce Homo: How One*

Becomes What One Is, completed shortly before he descended into the insanity that lasted until his death (1888).

> I have absolutely no knowledge of atheism as an outcome of reasoning, still less as an event; with me it is obviously by instinct (2014).

Nietzsche's bold, infamous declaration, "God is dead," is more a sociological statement than a theological assertion (1974, 95). He did not believe in a literal God who once lived and then died. Rather, he believed the failure of human beings to live as though they believed in God rendered religious faith meaningless and God functionally dead.

> "Whither is God?" he (the madman) cried, "I shall tell you. We have killed him - you and I. All of us are his murderers ... God is dead ... And we have killed him. How shall we, the murderers of all murderers, comfort ourselves?" (95).

For Nietzsche, "the end of Christianity (meant) the advent of nihilism" (Craig, 2008, 77). For centuries humankind had depended on God for a moral code to effect social order. Without God there is no authority for a code of conduct binding upon all human beings. A statement attributed to Fyodor Dostoevsky describes this situation: "If God does not exist then all things are possible" (2014). Nietzsche posited if God or some other absolute moral authority does not exist then we are left with moral anarchy. Nevertheless, he saw something redemptive emerging from this moral chaos: each of us bears responsibility for constructing and living out a self-determined morality. In *Beyond Good and Evil* he wrote:

As I was wandering through the many subtle and crude moralities that have been dominant or still dominate over the face of the earth, I found ... In the end, two basic types apparent to me and a fundamental distinction leaped out. There is a master morality and a slave morality (1966, 260).

Nietzsche rejected moral absolutism because it required both the strong and weak to adhere to the same ethical standards. He referred to the strong as "the noble" and the weak as "the herd." He strongly objected to the imposition of "the herd's" values upon "the noble." This imposition serves the interests of the weak, who benefit from the so-called virtues of selflessness and charity. The weak solicit help from the strong, using religion as leverage in making their appeal. "The noble" have the strength to impose their will on the weak and should do so, not allowing religion to restrain them.

Nietzsche also referred to "the noble" as the *Ubermenschen*, translated variously as the "overmen" or "supermen." The philosophy of the *Ubermenschen* was part of the 1924 murder trial of two wealthy University of Chicago law students, Nathan Leopold and Richard Loeb. On May 21, 1924 they abducted 14 year-old Bobby Frank, bludgeoned him with a chisel, and stuffed his body in a culvert. It was presented at trial that Leopold and Loeb were enthralled by Nietzsche's idea that society's concepts of good and evil do not apply to those who have the temerity to rise above social expectations. It was not so much the idea of murder that attracted them, but the idea of getting away with murder as a demonstration of their superior intellect and boldness.

Their defense attorney, Clarence Darrow, entered a plea of guilty in order to proceed to the sentencing phase and argue before the judge rather than the jury. Darrow was hopeful of a ruling of life sentences rather than executions. His eloquent twelve-hour argument included,

> Is any blame attached because somebody took Nietzsche's philosophy seriously and fashioned a life upon it? ... it is hardly fair to hang a 19 year-old boy for the philosophy that was taught him at a university (Darrow, 08/22/24).

In *Thus Spake Zarathustra: A Book for All and None* (1976) Nietzsche speaks through an aged prophet, replete with wisdom. The sage presents one of Nietzsche's most important ideas: "eternal recurrence." Presented as a hypothetical question, it asks: What if you were to live the life you are now living again and again throughout eternity - would this change you?

> What if some day or night, a demon were to steal after you into your loneliest loneliness and say to you: "This life as you now live it and have lived it, you will have to live once more and innumerable times more; and there will be nothing new in it, but every pain and every joy and every thought and sigh and everything unutterably small or great in your life will have to return to you, all in the same succession and sequence ... The eternal hourglass of existence is turned upside down again and again, and you with it, speck of dust!" Would you not throw yourself down and gnash your teeth and curse the demon who spoke thus? Or have you once experienced a tremendous moment when you would have answered him "You are a god and never have I heard anything more divine." If this thought gained possession of you, it would change you as you are or perhaps crush you (1976, 341).

Irvin Yalom, who is featured in chapter IX, has provided the following commentary on "eternal recurrence:"

> If you engage in this experiment and find the thought painful or even unbearable, there is one obvious explanation: you do not believe you've lived your life well. I would proceed by posing such questions as, How have you not lived well? What regrets do you have about your life?
> My purpose is not to draw anyone into a sea of regret for the past but, ultimately, to turn his or her gaze toward the future and this potentially life-changing question: *What can you do now in your life so that one year or five years from now, you won't look back and have similar dismay about the new regrets you've accumulated? In other words, can you find a way to live without continuing to accumulate regrets?* (2008, 101).

III. Karl Jaspers (1883-1969): *Science and Philosophy Blended*

The genuine scientist profits even from unjustified criticism. If he shrinks from criticism he has no genuine will to know.

- Karl Jaspers

The limits of science have always been the source of bitter disappointment when people expected something from science that it was not able to provide.

- Karl Jaspers

Karl Jaspers brought existentialism into the twentieth century by integrating the work of Soren Kierkegaard and Friedrich Nietzsche. By any standard, Jaspers was an extraordinary scholar. He studied law, following his father's profession, but switched to medicine. After a brief career as a psychiatrist, he accepted an appointment as a psychology professor. Ten years later, he redirected his attention to philosophy and eventually joined the faculty of the University of Basel in Switzerland. Working as an academic philosopher was ironic for Jaspers, who respected the writing of Kierkegaard and Nietzsche because they presented worldviews that were born of experience rather than academic reflection. In fact, Jaspers said of himself, "To decide to become a philosopher seemed as foolish to me as to decide to become a poet" (2014).

A theme in Jaspers' work that marks him as an existentialist is his insistence that an authentic life is possible only through decision-making and action. Although we do not choose to come into the world, he emphasized we can make decisions concerning what we need to do to become who we want to be. For Jaspers,

Descartes' *cogito* ("I think, therefore I am") addresses only basic existence, which objects have as well as human beings. Jaspers preferred to speak about *eligo* ("I choose") to stress the unique capability of human beings to seize their existence and transform it from "what is" to "what is possible."

In addition, he was sensitive to the challenge we face as individuals living in a mass society. For him, it is one thing to identity ourselves as part of a larger entity and quite another to define ourselves as individuals operating as free will agents. To identify ourselves nationally, as Americans; ethnically, as Germans; politically, as Democrats; or sexually, as males, is tantamount to denying responsibility for our thoughts and actions. For this reason he expressed contempt for the term "public opinion," which he considered an illusion:

> The 'public' is a phantom, the phantom of an opinion supposed to exist in a vast number of persons who have no effective interrelation ... Such an opinion is spoken of as 'public opinion,' a fiction which is appealed to by individuals and by groups as supporting their special views. It is impalpable, illusory, transient; ... a nullity which can nevertheless for a moment endow the multitude with power to uplift or destroy (2014).

Because his wife was Jewish, he was designated by the National Socialist Party as having a "Jewish taint." This led to his dismissal from his professorship at the University of Heidelberg. In 1937 he presented a series of lectures before The German Academy of Frankfurt entitled "Philosophy of Existence." Reflecting on the political and social situation of that time, Jaspers summarized his philosophy with these words:

In this total threat, I tried to pay homage to reason, to be bound to the sciences, to become aware of what was essential, and to think in the ground of all being (1971, v).

Two principle paths to knowledge are *rationalism* and *empiricism*. The former regards reason as the most reliable source of knowledge; the latter regards the scientific method as the most dependable route to truth. Since Jaspers did not see *rationalism* and *empiricism* in conflict he was able to view philosophy and science as potentially collaborative in the pursuit of knowledge. He valued science as the only reliable means for establishing *certain types* of knowledge. In his 1937 lecture he said, "Only the sciences can teach me to know the *way things are*. If the philosopher had no current knowledge of the sciences, he would remain without clear knowledge of the world, like a blind man" (1971, 11).

Nevertheless, more than any other existentialist, he insisted on the importance of clarifying the limitations of the scientific method. Trained as a physician, he was well-qualified to evaluate the capacity of science for ascertaining knowledge. He posited that any scientific premise that cannot be demonstrated by the scientific method is therefore not scientific. Thus he refuted the premise that the senses are the most reliable source of knowledge and asserted science's fundamental premise is actually a philosophical assumption. Rene Descartes addressed this issue over two centuries earlier when he hypothesized an "evil demon" who deceives the senses by presenting an external world that is a complete illusion.

Perhaps it was his diversity of training and experience that compelled Jaspers to value *empiricism* and *rationalism* along with *intuitionalism*. What **is** truth? Truth **is** what actually **is**. Each of these three paths to truth has an element of uncertainty. Scientists must carry on their work mindful that the senses can be deceived. Optical illusions, social pressure, and the placebo effect demonstrate the fallibility of sensory experience.

Philosophers must be mindful that even flawless logic is misleading when it is based on a false assumption. This makes it possible to reason correctly and still reach an incorrect conclusion. David Foster Wallace's 2005 commencement address at Kenyon College includes an anecdote illustrating this point. He told a story of an atheist and believer arguing about the existence of God. The atheist told of a time he was lost in an Alaskan blizzard and, fearing for his life, prayed to God for help. The believer, noting the atheist was alive to tell the story, said, "Well then, you must believe now" (2009, 24). The atheist responded, "No man, all that happened was a couple of Eskimos just happened to come wandering by, and they showed me the way back to camp" (24). The believer countered that it was God who sent the Eskimos in response to the atheist's prayer. Wallace used this story to illustrate:

> The exact same experience can mean two completely different things to two different people, given those people's two different belief templates and two different ways of constructing meaning from experience (24).

Intuition is knowledge derived from neither experience nor reasoning. Intuitive knowledge seems innate, as Carl Jung and evolutionary psychologists would have us to believe. It is what Blaise Pascal had in mind when he said, "Le coeur a ses raisons que raison ne connait pas" ("The heart has its reasons of which reason knows nothing") (2014). Nevertheless, even intensely felt intuitions can be in conflict. A man approaching a woman feeling she is the who one fate intends for him while she feels destined for someone else is a mundane illustration of conflicting intuitions.

Jaspers respected all three paths to knowledge and believed them integral to life management. As with any existentialist, he believed what we do is more defining than what we know or how we came to know it. He wrote, "We not do merely exist; rather our existence is entrusted to us as the arena and the body for the realization of our origin" (Jaspers, 1971, 4).

IV. Martin Heidegger (1889-1976): *Being Towards Death*

Self-awareness is a supreme gift, a treasure as precious as life. This is what makes us human. But it comes with a costly price: the wound of mortality. Our existence is forever shadowed by the knowledge that we will grow, blossom, and inevitably, diminish and die.

- Irvin Yalom

In contrast to Karl Jaspers, Martin Heidegger retained his university position. He did so because of his membership in the Nazi Party and what appears to have been support for Adolf Hitler. These associations do not mean Heidegger approved of the Holocaust or actually favored the politics and programs of the Nazi regime. Possibly, his support was insincere and intended only to retain his professorship. Also possible is Heidegger, like many German citizens, favored the National Socialist Party only in its early years. After World War II Jaspers advocated the removal of Heidegger from his teaching position at the University of Freiberg. Heidegger continues to be a controversial figure and as recently as 1997 a book was published that explores his Nazi affiliation (Young, 1997).

Immanuel Kant, an eighteenth century German philosopher, encapsulated the study of philosophy as the attempt to answer four questions. One of these questions is, "What is a human being?" Before considering Heidegger's philosophy of death, attention must be given to his concepts of a human being and *thrownness*.

Heidegger referred to human beings using the word *Dasein*, which literally means "Being-there." To be human is to be "there," with "there" being the world. He believed if human beings are to be understood they must be considered as beings existing in the world surrounded by other things. The world is here, now, and everywhere around us. We are immersed in it. In fact, how could we be anywhere else? We are engrossed by the world as our senses perceive it and engaged in an ongoing effort to make sense of our experiences.

Characterizing us as "Beings-in-the-World" went beyond Descartes' description of us as merely "beings that think." Heidegger elaborated by addressing some of the things we think about: *Who am I? Is there a meaning to my life? Is death the end of my existence?* Pondering these questions generates anxiety, which is the natural condition of human beings (Menand, 2014). Further, these questions raise other questions giving rise to even more anxiety. Perhaps life is absurd. What if there is no meaning to life except the meaning I determine for myself? Besides, I did not ask to be born and now I am in an unchosen situation with innumerable other conditions not of my choosing. I have been thrown into the world. Heidegger referred to this as *thrownness* and its meaning was grasped by Jim Morrison of The Doors in the last song he recorded, "Riders on the Storm."

> Riders on the storm
> Riders on the storm,
> Into this house were born
> Into this world we're thrown.
> Like a dog without a bone
> An actor out on loan,

Riders on the storm (1971).

A few, like David Benetar, have extrapolated from *thrownness* the proposition of *antinatalism*, the belief that it is immoral to have children because they are not consulted about their entrance into the world. Since life includes considerable pain, pleasure notwithstanding, we are *Better Never to Have Been* (2006).

Perhaps the most important of our experiences is death. We observe the death of others with the awareness that it awaits us. Viktor Frankl, the subject of the next chapter, included death as one of life's three inevitable, but redeemable, tragedies. Although life is temporary and fleeting, Frankl believed we have the potential to derive "from life's transitoriness an incentive to take responsible action" (1959, 162). Heidegger believed the same. In his first scholarly book, *Being and Time* (1927), he characterized living with the knowledge of death as "Being Towards Death." In spite of this phrase's grim implication,

> There is nothing morbid about being-towards-death. Heidegger's thought is that being-towards-death pulls Dasein out of its immersion in inauthentic everyday life and allows it come into its own. It is only in relation to being-towards-death that I become passionately aware of my freedom (Critchley, 07/13/2009).

In spite of our potential for using death to our advantage, he saw in us the tendency to suppress our thoughts about death, making it less threatening.

> (Death) is understood as an indefinite something which, above all, must arrive from somewhere or another, but

which is proximally not yet present-at-hand for oneself, and is therefore no threat (1962, 297).

Heidegger posited although death is certain, our suppression of thoughts about our own death renders it *non-relational* and *indefinite*. It is *non-relational* because we cannot experience it through the death of someone else, regardless of how close to us that person might have been. It is *indefinite* because we do not know the time and place of our own death, making it difficult to envision.

For Heidegger, "Being Towards Death" is necessary for living an authentic life. He wrote contemptuously of its opposite - an inauthentic life, which he referred to as *Das Man - a mindless following of the herd*. To live inauthentically is to live an unexamined life, devoid of introspection, which Socrates characterized as a life not worth living. The individual who lives inauthentically is "not oneself" but an impersonal "they" (1962, 164). The Quaker theologian David Elton Trueblood recognized the seriousness of an inauthentic life and concluded:

> It is surely not so bad to die, providing one has really lived before he dies. Life need not be long to be good, for indeed it cannot be long. The tragedy is not that all die, but that so many fail to really live (1951, 164).

V.   Viktor Frankl (1905-1997): *Tragic Optimism*

When we are no longer able to change a situation we are challenged to change ourselves.

- Viktor Frankl

Happiness cannot be pursued; it must be ensued. One must have a reason to "be happy." Once the reason is found, however, one becomes happy automatically.

- Viktor Frankl

It is not an overstatement to claim that Viktor Frankl has left a larger imprint on the world than any other existential philosopher. A Holocaust survivor, his memoir, *Man's Search for Meaning* (1959) is a classic in the fields of philosophy and psychiatry. Translated into twenty-four languages, it has sold over twelve million copies. The Library of Congress and Book-of-the-Month Club have declared it one of the ten most influential books in American literary history. Commenting on his magnum opus, Frankl reflected:

> I wrote the book in 1945 (and) did so in nine successive days ... I wanted to simply convey to the reader by way of a concrete example that life holds a potential meaning under any conditions, even the most miserable ones. And I thought if the point of view were demonstrated in a situa-tion as extreme as a concentration camp, my book might gain a hearing. ... I thought it might be helpful to people who are prone to despair (1959, 16).

Neither is it an overstatement to claim is he is one of the twentieth century's greatest thinkers. Frankl was a practicing psychiatrist prior to his three-year internment in Nazi concentration camps. Following liberation, he earned a Ph.D. in philosophy. His doctoral dissertation, *The Unconscious God*, analyzes unconscious spirituality and the relationship between psychotherapy and theology (1948).

Frankl's credentials as an existentialist are unquestionable if you consider his thoughts concerning freedom, responsibility, life's meaning, and decision-making as expressed in his writing:

> I recommend that the Statue of Liberty on the East Coast be supplemented by a Statue of Responsibility on the West Coast (1959, 156).

> What matters, therefore, is not the meaning of life in general but rather the specific meaning of a person's life at a given moment. To put the question in general terms would be comparable to the question posed to a chess master: "Tell me, Master, what is the best move in the world?" There is no such thing as the best move or even a good move apart from a particular situation in a game (1959, 131).

> Today education cannot afford to proceed along the lines of tradition, but must elicit the ability to make independent and authentic decisions. In an age in which the Ten Commandments seem to lose their unconditional validity, man must learn more than ever to listen to the ten thousand commandments arising from the ten thousand unique situations of which life consists (1964, 64-65).

Tragic Optimism

In the epilogue to *Man's Search for Meaning*, Frankl advanced one of his most important ideas: *Tragic Optimism*. He introduced this idea with these words:

> Let us first ask ourselves what should be understood by "a tragic optimism." In brief it means that one is, and remains, optimistic in spite of the "tragic triad," as it is called in (existential) therapy, a triad which consists of those aspects of human existence which may be circumscribed by: (1) pain; (2) guilt; and (3) death.... How is it possible to say yes to life in spite of all that? How, to pose the question differently, can life retain its potential meaning in spite of its tragic aspects? (1959, 161).

Frankl believed there are three unavoidable tragedies in life: pain, guilt, and death. He opted for the word "optimism" because he also believed in the human potential to make "the best" of each of these tragedies. (The Latin word *optimum* means "the best.") This potential allows for:

> (1) turning suffering into a human achievement and accomplishment; (2) deriving from guilt the opportunity to change oneself for the better; and (3) deriving from life's transitoriness an incentive to take responsible action (162).

As might be expected, concerning pain he quoted Friedrich Nietzsche: "That which does not kill me makes me stronger" (103). Even in the midst of a concentration camp he encouraged himself and others with the thought that, "Whatever we had gone through could still be an asset to us in the future" (103). A benefit of pain is its capacity for fostering compassion. The poet Betty Sue Flowers addressed this idea eloquently when she wrote, "Pain is a mechanism for growth, it carves out the heart to make room for compassion" (Cronkite, 1994, 315).

Frankl viewed guilt as an asset if it is not prolonged beyond its use. He saw it as a tool for committing or recommitting to being a better person. Oscar Wilde rightly observed, "No man is rich enough to buy back his past" (Malikow, 2014, 31). Professional boxing legend Muhammed Ali exemplifies the redemptive use of guilt with this reflection on his earlier years:

> I used to chase women all the time. And I won't say it was right, but look at all the temptations I had. I was young, handsome, heavyweight champion of the world. Women were always offering themselves to me. I had two children by women I wasn't married to. I love them; they're my children. I feel just as good and proud of them as I do my other children, but it wasn't the right thing to do. And running around, living that kind of life, wasn't good for me. It hurt my wife, it offended God. It never really made me happy. But ask any man who's forty years old – if he knew at twenty what he knows now, would he do things different? Most people would. So I did wrong; I'm sorry. And all I'll say as far as running around chasing women is concerned, is that's all past. I've got a good wife now, and I'm lucky to have her (37).

Since Ali has expressed regret for his womanizing and apologized to the people he hurt he is in a position to forgive himself. Aristotle's *principle of the golden mean* teaches moral excellence is the apex between two extremes. In Ali's case, one extreme would have him denying that he did anything wrong or hurt anybody. Such denial would be sociopathic. The other extreme would be obsessing over his wrongdoing and a life of guilt and shame culminating in suicide. Between these extremes is where you find Ali – responsible, remorseful, and appreciative of his present circumstances. This is what Frankl had in mind when speaking of optimizing guilt.

For Frankl, even death can be redemptive when it provokes praiseworthy action. He strenuously disagreed with Sigmund Freud, who believed imminent death brings out the worst in people. Expressing his disagreement, Frankl wrote:

> Sigmund Freud once asserted, "Let one attempt to expose a number of the most diverse people uniformly to hunger. With the increase of the imperative urge of hunger all individual differences will blur, and in their stead will appear the uniform expression of the one unstilled urge." Thank heaven, Sigmund Freud was spared knowing the concentration camps from the inside. His subjects lay on a couch designed in the plush style of Victorian culture, not the filth of Auschwitz. There, the "individual differences" did not "blur" but, on the contrary, people became more different; people unmasked themselves, both the swine and the saints (1959, 178).

Frankl believed, "A human being is a deciding being" with the capacity to make decisions even when death is fast approaching (2014). The determination to act honorably when facing death is to "make the most" of death.

VI. Jean-Paul Sartre (1905-1980): *Condemned to Be Free*

Freedom is what you do with what's been done to you.

- Jean-Paul Sartre

Commitment is an act, not a word.

- Jean-Paul Sartre

Because of his expression, "Existence precedes essence," no one is more associated with existentialism than Jean-Paul Sartre (1957, 13). To claim *existence precedes essence* is to postulate an individual's true character is defined by the actions that constitute that person's life. Sartre maintained, "Man is ... nothing else than the ensemble of his acts, nothing else than his life" (32). From this it follows that Sartre rejected the concept of *human nature*, which is to say he believed we have no identity merely because we are human beings. For each of us, identity is declared by our actions. In his celebrated lecture, *Existentialism is a Humanism* he affirmed, "man first of all exists, encounters himself, surges up in the world - and defines himself afterwards" (2014).

In the ironic statement, "Man is condemned to be free," Sartre expressed his belief that we fear our own freedom (1957, 23). Why? Because as free persons we must accept complete responsibility for our choices and their subsequent consequences. "And this is a circumstance that most of us find, at least some of the time completely overwhelming" (Wartenberg, 2010, 39). In his play, *The Flies* (1947), Sartre retells the story of *Oresteia* (Aeschylus, 458

B.C.). In Sartre's version, in a debate with Zeus, the ruler of the
Olympian gods, Orestes takes delight in his freedom:

> Orestes (to Zeus): You are the king of gods, king of stones
> and stars, king of waves of the sea. But you are not the king
> of man.
> Zeus: Impudent spawn! So I am not your king? Who, then,
> made you?
> Orestes: You. But you blundered; you should not have
> made me free.
> Zeus: I gave you freedom that you might serve me.
> Orestes: Perhaps. But now it has turned against the giver.
> And neither you nor I can undo what has been done.
> Zeus: Ah, at last! So this is your excuse?
> Orestes: I am not excusing myself.
> Zeus: No? Let me tell you it sounds much like an excuse,
> this freedom whose slave you claim to be.
> Orestes: Neither slave nor master. I am my freedom. No
> sooner had you created me then I ceased to be yours (*The
> Flies*, III, 120-121).

"A knife ... is not responsible cutting someone, it is the
person who wields it who bears the responsibility. Similarly, If we
were truly just Zeus' minions, it would be he - and not we - who
would be responsible for our actions" (Wartneberg, 2010, 39).
Sartre, an atheist, used the illustration of a paper cutter to make the
point that its creator had the cutting of paper in mind when
designing and constructing it. Its structure is its essence. In contrast
to paper cutters, human beings have no creator and, therefore, have
no predetermined nature. Our defining characteristics emanate from
our actions, which are self-determined. In *Existentialism and Human
Emotions* not only did he say "man is free," he added, "man is

freedom" (1957, 23). Sartre then proceeded to explain why our freedom is also our severe punishment:

> I say that man is condemned to be free. Condemned, because he did not create himself, yet in other respects free; because, once thrown into the world, he is responsible for everything he does (23).

In addition, it is our responsibility to manage our emotions, regardless of how powerful they might be.

> The existentialist does not believe in the power of passion. He will never agree that a sweeping passion is a ravaging torrent which fatally leads a man to certain acts and is therefore an excuse. He thinks that man is responsible for his passion (23).

Even if the passion to be managed is love, we must be its master rather than its slave. Sartre disagreed with the sentiment of the poet Robert Frost, who defined love as, "the irresistible desire to be desired irresistibly" (1911). Moreover, Sartre viewed love as a form of slavery:

> So prevalent is this tendency for people to reduce one another to the status of objects that they mange to do so even when in love. When people love someone they say they want what what is best for the beloved. Now the highest fulfillment of man's existence is to be free, so if a person loves another he should want that person to be free. Yet one of the first things a person tries to do when he is in love is to take his beloved's freedom away. One wants the person he loves to belong to him (Katen, 1973, 201).

No doubt, Sartre would have found Shakespeare's characterization of love more agreeable: "Love is not love which alters. ... Love alters not with his brief hours and weeks. But bears it out to the edge of doom. If this be error and upon me proved, I never writ, nor man ever loved" (Sonnet 116).

Neither did Sartre consider social influences to be irresistible. He maintained that nothing outside of us compels us to act a certain way.

> Thus there are no *accidents* in life; a community event which suddenly bursts forth and involves me in it does not come from the outside. If I am mobilized in a war, this war is *my* war; it is in my image and I deserve it. I deserve it first because I could always get out of it by suicide or by desertion; these ultimate possibles are those which must always be present for us when there is a question of envisaging a situation. For lack of getting out of it, I have *chosen* it (1957, 54).

Bad Faith is Sartre's term for disowning our own values and adopting society's false values. Since this occurs unconsciously it is a form of self-deception.

As stated above, Sartre was an atheist. However, he was not militant about his unbelief, largely because he believed even the existence of God would not negate human responsibility. Regarding this position, he wrote: "Existentialism isn't so atheistic that it wears itself out showing that God doesn't exist. Rather, it declares that even if God did exist, that would change nothing" (51). With or without God, freedom is simultaneously a blessing and burden. A blessing because we have dominion over our own lives, thereby deciding many of the conditions that affect us. A burden because ultimately we are accountable for the outcome of our decisions.

Hell Is Other People

In Sartre's play, *No Exit* (1944), three characters find themselves in hell, perfectly suited to be each other's tormentor. Their fate is to spend a sleepless eternity together in one small room. Understandably, one of them eventually says, "Hell is other people." Concerning this celebrated quotation, Sartre maintained it often has been misunderstood:

> It has been thought that what I meant by that was that our relations with other people are always poisoned, that they are invariably hellish relations. But what I really mean is something totally different. I mean that if relations with someone else are twisted, vitiated, then that other person can only be hell. Why? Because ... when we think about ourselves, when we try to know ourselves, ... we use the knowledge of us which other people already have. ...Into whatever I say about myself someone else's judgment always enters. (Woodward, 2010).

Being-for-Others is Sartre's term for the effect others have on us with their looks and judgments. "Hell is other people" when we evaluate ourselves by looking to others. The "Riddle of the Coal Miners" illustrates the danger of doing this:

> At the end of the work day two coal miners emerge from the mine. One has a clean face, the other a face blackened with coal soot. They look at each other, say good day, and go to their respective homes. The miner with the clean face washes his face before eating his dinner. The miner with the dirty face doesn't wash his face before sitting for dinner.

> Question: Why did the man with the clean face wash and the man with the dirty face not wash? Answer: Each man looked at the other and assumed since we came from the same place (the coal mine), my face must look like his.

It is no wonder Sartre declared, "I hate victims who respect their executioners" (2014).

VII. Simone de Beauvoir (1908-1986): *Ethical Ambiguity*

I tore myself away from the safe comfort of certainties through my love for truth - and truth rewarded me.

- Simone de Beauvoir

It is fitting that Simone de Beauvoir is buried next to Jean-Paul Sartre since their lives and work were intertwined. They met at the University of Paris in 1929 and remained as lovers and collaborators until Sartre's death in 1980. In her novelized version of a part of their life together, she described their relationship with these words: "You and I are simply one. That is the truth. Neither of us can be described without the other" (Cogswell, 2008, 131). She contributed to Sartre's work by reading his manuscripts before they were sent on to be published and he did the same for her.

A versatile writer, de Beauvoir produced novels as well non-fiction works on philosophical, political, and social issues. Her 1945 novel, *Le Sang des Autres* (*The Blood of Others*), a love story set in war-torn France, was made into a movie in 1984 starring Jodie Foster and Sam Neill. *The Second Sex* (1949) addresses the treatment of women throughout history and paved the way for the 1960's and 70's feminist movement. Her philosophical treatise, *The Ethics of Ambiguity* (1954), is perhaps the best-known discourse on existentialist ethics. Even Sartre, a prolific writer, did not produce a monograph on this topic in spite of his promise to do so.

The Ethics of Ambiguity

In *The Ethics of Ambiguity* de Beauvoir reiterates the fundamental existentialist premise that our nature is created by our choices and subsequent actions ("existence precedes essence"). She also agreed with Heidegger that we create ourselves in the present by reflecting on our past and projecting ourselves into the future. And since we cannot fully know the future effects of our present choices, we feel the weight of every significant decision we contemplate. This is a burden we cannot escape because to be human is to have free will.

Regarding freedom, she made a distinction between *ontological freedom* and *moral freedom*. The former is the freedom that comes with being human. Therefore, ironically, we cannot escape being free. The latter is volitional, meaning we can choose to act *amorally*. (There is a difference between being *amoral* and *immoral*. The amoral person is unprincipled and unconcerned with rightness or wrongness. The immoral person is concerned with rightness or wrongness but does not conform to the accepted standards of morality.) When de Beauvoir wrote, "to will oneself moral and to will oneself free are one in the same decision," she meant that moral freedom is derived from ontological freedom (1954, 24).

She maintained that since our values are largely expressed by our behavior towards others, it is through relationships that we disclose who we are. "To will oneself free is also to will others free" expresses her belief that the guiding principle in our relationships should be acting to maximize the freedom of others as well holding them responsible for their actions (73). She emphasized since we cannot completely know what the results of our choices will be, we can never be certain an action is right while contemplating it. However, although we cannot know the specific outcome of a choice, we can accurately estimate whether that choice will contribute to our own or another person's freedom. Hence, a corollary to her guiding principle is treating others as we ourselves would desire to be treated.

For example, consider a man who had an extramarital affair. Although the affair was brief and occurred many years ago, he still feels guilty and is contemplating telling his wife about it. This creates a dilemma for him: telling her would cause her great pain but not telling her will perpetuate his guilt. After wrestling with this quandary he confessed to his wife. His wife determined she does not want to be married to an adulterer and divorced him. Although his confession resulted in an undesirable outcome, his wife's freedom was honored. De Beauvoir asserted a desirable outcome is not required for an action to advance the moral freedom of another person. As stated above, she conceded there is no certainty of a favorable outcome in the exercise of moral freedom. What we can determine is if our actions will contribute to the freedom of others. Therefore, we should make a sincere effort to act in ways that allow others to make unhindered choices, enabling them to take responsibility for their actions.

In the conclusion of *The Ethics of Ambiguity* de Beauvoir expressed her belief that our own freedom depends on each of us acting to preserve the freedom of others: "Since the individual is defined only by his relationship to the world and to other individuals; he exists only by transcending himself, and his freedom can be achieved only through the freedom of others" (156). Her assertion that right moral choices require acknowledgment of other people as free moral agents addressed the frequently heard criticism that existentialism is *ethically relativistic*. (*Ethical relativism* is the idea that there are no universal moral standards, making "right" and "wrong" merely a matter of an individual's opinion.) The idea that authentic moral decision-making requires concern for the freedom of others provides an objective criterion for determining whether a choice or action is moral. Commenting on *The Ethics of Ambiguity*, Professor Charlotte Moore has written:"There's no such thing as the opinion of an isolated individual, because there's no such thing as an isolated individual. For these reasons, de Beauvoir's *Ethics of Ambiguity* contradicts the very definition of ethical subjectivism" (2014).

VIII. Albert Camus (1913-1960): *Philosophy's One Question*

The only way to deal with an unfree world is to become so absolutely free that your very existence is an act of rebellion.

- Albert Camus

In 1948 Albert Camus, an atheist, was invited by the Dominican monks of Latour-Maubourg to address them on the topic: "What Unbelievers Expect from Christians." Sensing honesty in their assurance that they were not seeking to engage him in a debate, he accepted the invitation. As one would anticipate from an existentialist, he told them he expected Christians to:

> get away from abstraction and confront the blood-stained face history has taken on today. The grouping we need is a grouping of men resolved to speak out clearly and pay up personally (Blackburn, 2011).

In addition, he expected Christians to take action to alleviate human suffering, especially when it cannot be eradicated: "Perhaps we cannot prevent this world from being a world in which children are tortured. But we can reduce the number of tortured children" (2011). This expectation is consistent with one of the themes of his novel, *The Plague* (1947), in which one of the characters, Dr.Rieux, exhaustedly works to combat a plague knowing he is laboring in a lost cause. Camus was awarded the Nobel Peace Prize for Literature in 1957, three years before his death in an automobile accident. There is an element of irony in the accident that took his life. In his pocket was an unused train ticket to the same place to which he was being driven. At the last minute he changed his travel arrangements.

Immanuel Kant encapsulated philosophy as the pursuit of answers to four questions:

1. What can we know?
2. What can we hope for?
3. How should we behave?
4. What is a human being?

Camus was even more expeditious:

> There is but one truly serious philosophical problem, and that is suicide. Judging whether life is or is not worth living amounts to answering the fundamental question of philosophy (1955, 3).

With this assertion Camus was not encouraging suicide any more than Socrates was when he said, "The unexamined life is not worth living" (*Apology*, 38a). By their statements both men are calling us to a carefully considered life. For Socrates this meant the richest life available (Greek *eudaimonia*) is a life of contemplation directed toward understanding why we think, act, and feel as we do. For Camus this meant identifying what gives our life meaning such that we choose to go on living. Gordon Livingston has incorporated both ideas into his work as a psychiatrist:

> When confronted with a suicidal person I seldom try to talk them out of it. Instead I ask them to examine what it is that has so far dissuaded them from killing themselves. Usually this involves finding out what the connections are that tether that person to life in the face of nearly unbearable psychic pain (2004, 71-72).

Of course, this raises the question: What if the patient can not discover any connections that tether him to life? In Dr. Livingston's experience this has rarely occurred: "In thirty-three years of practicing psychiatry I have lost this argument only once" (72). Notwithstanding, undoubtedly Shakespeare's Macbeth spoke for others in this dour soliloquy:

> Tomorrow, and tomorrow, and tomorrow,
> Creeps in this petty pace from day to day
> To the last syllable of recorded time,
> And all our yesterdays have lighted fools
> The way to dusty death. Out, out, brief candle!
> Life's but a walking shadow, a poor player
> That struts and frets his hour upon the stage
> And then is heard no more. It is a tale
> Told by an idiot, full of sound and fury,
> Signifying nothing (*Macbeth*, Act V, scene 5).

The Myth of Sisyphus

Camus began his renown essay, "The Myth of Sisyphus," with a description of the eternal fate of Sisyphus, the King of Ephyra, who antagonized the gods with his passion for life and hatred of death.

> The gods had condemned Sisyphus to ceaselessly rolling a rock to the top of a mountain, whence the stone would fall back of its own weight. They had thought with some reason that there is no more dreadful punishment than futile and hopeless labor (1955, 88).

Simone de Beauvoir showed her agreement with the gods when she wrote: "There is no more obnoxious way to punish a man than to force him to perform acts which make no sense to him, as when one empties and fills the same ditch indefinitely, when one makes soldiers who are being punished march up and down, when one forces a schoolboy to copy lines" (2014). Camus used Sisyphus as a metaphor for the repetitive tasks that constitute life for the workingman. In this vein he wrote:

> If this myth is tragic, that is because its hero is conscious. Where would his torture be, indeed, if at every step the hope of succeeding upheld him. The workingman of today works everyday in his life at the same tasks, and this fate is no less absurd. But it is tragic only at the rare moments when it becomes conscious (1955, 88-90).

Thomas Nagel has expressed a similar idea concerning the absurdity of life. He believes, "(We) vacillate between two different perspectives on our own activities. When we are involved in doing something, we normally think we are doing something worthwhile" (Wartenberg, 2008, 120). However, a second perspective invades our thinking and belittles our labor:

> If I'm a violinist, I have to think there's something signifi-cant about playing the violin or I won't be able to engage in the strenuous practice required to become skilled. ... If I think about the fact that I am just one human being on a planet in one solar system in a vast galaxy that is but a small part of an unimaginably huge universe, my own violin play-ing just won't seem something that makes a difference at all (120).

Surprisingly, Camus concluded, "One must imagine Sisyphus as happy" (1955, 91).Why? Because he recognizes the absurdity of life; he is fully aware it is futile "to demand reasonableness of a universe that does not, that cannot provide it (Wartenberg, 115). Sisyphus labors at the work from which he cannot escape without the delusion that a blissful life awaits him at a future time in another place. Unlike those who yearn for heaven, he knows, "Life is a long preparation for something that never happens" (Yeats, 2014).

An existential prescription for this absurdity is provided by Walt Whitman's poem, "O Me! O Life!"

O Me! O life! ... of the questions of these recurring;
Of the endless trains of the faithless - of cities fill'd with the foolish;
Of myself forever reproaching myself, (for who more foolish than I, and who more faithless?)
Of the eyes that vainly crave the light - of the objects mean - of the struggle ever renew'd;
Of the poor results of all - of the plodding and sordid crowds I see around me;
Of the empty and useless years of the rest - with the rest me intertwined;
The question, O me! so sad, recurring - What good amid these, O me, O life?

Answer
That you are here - that life exists, and identity;
That the powerful play goes on, and you will contribute a verse (1900).

Camus saw Sisyphus as heroic because he is not over-whelmed by his everlasting fate. In addition, Camus sees him as astute because he clearly understands that life is absurd. Of course, Sisyphus does not have the option of suicide, but this makes him all the more admirable. Unlike those who commit suicide, he is not overmatched by life. Camus addressed this difference: "In a sense, and as in melodrama, killing yourself amounts to confessing. It is confessing that life is too much for you or that you do not understand it (1955, 5). Camus concludes his essay with a tribute to Sisyphus:

> I leave Sisyphus at the foot of the mountain! One always finds one's burden again. But Sisyphus teaches the higher fidelity that negates the gods and raises rocks. He too concludes that all is well. This universe henceforth without a master seems to him neither sterile nor futile. Each atom of that stone, each mineral flake of that night-filled mountain, in itself forms a world. The struggle itself towards the heights is enough to fill a man's heart. One must imagine Sisyphus happy (1955, 91).

Sisyphus is not seeking the meaning of life. Rather, he is living the life he has, such as it is. Camus, who wrote, "You will never live if you are looking for the meaning of life," found this commendable (2014).

IX. Irvin Yalom (1931 - the present):
Psychotherapy's Two Questions and Four Issues

No positive change can occur in your life as long as you cling to the thought that the reason for your not living well lies outside yourself. ... And even if you face overwhelming external restraints, you still have the freedom and the choice of adopting various attitudes toward those restraints.

- Irvin Yalom

Like Karl Jaspers and Viktor Frankl, Irvin Yalom is both a psychiatrist and philosopher. Like Simone de Beauvoir and Jean-Paul Sartre, Yalom is a versatile writer. His novels integrate psychotherapy and philosophy. (One of his novels, *When Nietzsche Wept*, was made into a movie in 2007, with Armand Assante portraying Friedrich Nietzsche.) His clinical manual, *Theory and Practice of Group Psychotherapy* (2005) is the standard text for mental health professionals. Although Frankl is the founder of existential therapy, it is Yalom who has written the classic textbook on the subject (1980). In addition, he is a Professor Emeritus of Psychiatry at Stanford University.

Psychotherapy's Two Questions

Few clinicians have written as extensively and profoundly as Yalom on the subject of psychotherapy. He begins *Love's Executioner*, a collection of case studies, with a striking confession:

> I do not like to work with patients who are in love. Perhaps it is because of envy - I, too, crave enchantment. Perhaps it is because love and psychotherapy are incompatible. The good therapist fights darkness and seeks illumination, while

romantic love is sustained by mystery and crumbles upon inspection. I hate to be love's executioner (1989, 15).

In this book he provides a two-question, existential characterization of psychotherapy. For all its complexity, Yalom believes psychotherapy can be reduced to two questions: *What does the patient really want?* and, *Is the patient's current lifestyle compatible with what she has said she really wants?*

Concerning the first question, he has written: "Could anything be simpler? One innocent question and its answer. And yet, time after time, I have seen this group exercise evoke unexpectedly powerful feelings" (3). One of the powerful feelings he has observed is pain - existence pain. It is the pain that is "whirring just beneath the membrane of life" (3). It is the pain that can be provoked by "a few minutes of deep reflection, a work of art, a sermon, a personal crisis, a loss" (4). It is the pain that arises from one of two realizations. One is our desire for something that is impossible - a halt to aging, the return of a deceased loved one, some achievement, perhaps even immortality itself. The second is the realization that our lifestyle is incompatible with what we say we really want.

Both of these realizations are existential issues. If we desire something unattainable, we are left to fashion a life in accordance with those things that are attainable. No one can determine for us what form such a life will take. It is our responsibility to decide and act. If we realize our manner of living is inconsistent with what we claim we really want then we have two options. Either we change our claim to accommodate to our lifestyle or alter our lifestyle to be harmonious with our claim. Again, no one can make this choice for us.

Psychotherapy's Four Philosophical Issues

In Yalom's experience there are four philosophical issues present in psychotherapy. Sometimes they are addressed overtly, but more often they are discussed indirectly, moving like four currents beneath the water's surface. They are:

> The inevitability of death for each of us and for those we love; the freedom to make our lives as we will; our ultimate aloneness; and, finally, the absence of any obvious meaning or sense to life (1989, 4-5).

In philosophical jargon, these four issues are existence, free will and responsibility, life's meaning, and *existential isolation.*

Existence

Yalom has written, "our existence is forever shadowed by the knowledge that we will grow, blossom, and, inevitably, diminish and die" (2008, 1). He devoted an entire book to the inevitability of death, using the metaphor "staring at the sun" (2008). He believes just as we occasionally glimpse at the sun without staring at it, lest we go blind, we also glance at death because a long, fixed look at it would be too unsettling. In psychotherapy, the impermanence of existence is indirectly addressed by patients by expressing concern with how they are managing life - the one life of which they are certain.

Free Will and Responsibility

Is free will a reality or an illusion? While the free will - determinism debate rages on in philosophy, authentic choice-making is a given in psychotherapy. Psychiatrist Sue Chance's memoir,

Stronger Than Death: When Suicide Touches Your Life - a Mother's Story, is her reflection on the loss of her son to self-inflicted death. In the last chapter, she speaks of choice and responsibility:

> I also believe whatever failures of a parent or parents, the individual takes over his or her own destiny. In working with adolescents from very sick families, I finally decided the best thing I could do is give them the following lecture: "You want to tell me how much your parents messed up and how much pain they've caused you. I believe you. I know that your complaints are legitimate. But you're coming closer and closer to the time in your life when you can take over and make it better for yourself. That's going to be your choice: whether you stay stuck in blaming and moaning about all the things that have been unfair or get on with it and do the best you can with what you have.
>
> Kids don't like that message any better than adults do, any better than I did the first time I gave it to myself. But it has the utility of being true and ultimately helpful.
>
> I do not like my parents and I do not like the things they did to me. However, I am responsible for who I am now. There is no way I can reasonably say that, at forty-nine, I am more a product of the first fifteen years I spent with them than I am of the past thirty-four years I have spent with myself. I would, in fact, be very ashamed of myself if it were true (1992, 148).

Yalom agrees with her; in *Existential Psychotherapy* he wrote:

> Responsibility means authorship. To be aware of responsibility is to be aware of creating one's own self, destiny, life predicament, feelings, and, if such be the case, one's own suffering. For the patient who will not accept such responsibility, who persists in blaming others- either

other individuals or other forces - for his or her dysphoria (discontentment), no real therapy is possible (1980, 218).

Life's Meaning

Yalom is acutely aware of the dilemma implicit in the question: "What is the meaning of life?" On one hand he admits human beings require meaning - "firm ideals to which we can aspire and guidelines by which to steer our lives" (1980, 422). On the other hand, he asks, "How does a being who needs meaning find meaning in a meaningless universe?" (423).

He maintains values (How should I live?) are derived from meaning (Why should I live?) Human beings are not driven by instinct to act a certain way and, lacking a religious tradition, are not guided to behave in a certain manner. What remains is intuition - an unreasoned sense of how we should conduct ourselves and fill our lives. Like Frankl, he prefers the ten thousand commandments to the Ten Commandments:

> In an age in which the Ten Commandments seem to lose their unconditional validity, man must learn more than ever to listen to the ten thousand commandments arising from the ten thousand unique situations of which life consists (Frankl, 1964, 64-65).

Yalom concludes, "Meaning ensues from meaningful activity" (1989, 12).

> The search for meaning, much like the search for pleasure, must be conducted obliquely. ... In therapy, as in life, meaningfulness is a by-product of engagement and commitment, and that is where therapists must direct their

efforts - not that engagement provides the rational answer to questions of meaning, but it causes these questions not to matter (1989, 12).

Existential Isolation

"Existential isolation refers to an unbridgeable gulf between oneself and any other being. It refers, too, to an isolation even more fundamental - a separation between the individual and the world" (1980, 355). Recognizing the vagueness of the phrase, "a separation between the individual and the world," Yalom provides clarification by quoting one of his patients:

> Remember the movie "West Side Story," when the two lovers meet, and suddenly everything else in the world mystically fades away, and they are absolutely alone with one another? Well, that's what happens to me at these times. Except there's no one else there but me (355).

The experience of loneliness is common to all human beings. At times we feel it as alienation from others; at other times it is a sense of not knowing ourselves; at still other times it is detected as disconnection from our environment. Thomas Wolfe captured our alienation from others in one of his novels. In *Look Homeward Angel* (1929) the protagonist, Eugene Grant, muses on his loneliness and concludes: "(Men are) forever strangers to one another, that no one ever comes really to know anyone. ... no matter what arms may clasp us, what mouth may kiss us, what heart may warm us" (1929, 31). It is hardly surprising that another book, *Why Am I Afraid to Tell You Who I Am?* (Powell, 1969) has sold over 15 million copies and been translated into 22 languages.

Epilogue: *Nine Questions from Nine Existentialists*

As a summary and review of the preceding pages, listed below are nine conceivable questions from the philosophers considered in this primer.

1. Soren Kierkegaard: Do your actions give credibility to what you claim to believe?

2. Friedrich Nietzsche: Are you prepared to establish your own, personalized code of conduct?

3. Karl Jaspers: Do you have one, two or three paths to knowledge?

4. Martin Heidegger: Are you living with a continual awareness of your death?

5. Viktor Frankl: Are you making the most of life's three unavoidable tragedies: pain, guilt, and death?

6. Jean-Paul Sartre: Do you believe free will is a blessing, burden or both?

7. Simone de Beauvoir: Do you appreciate the ambiguity of ethics and the difficulty of ethical decision-making?

8. Albert Camus: What is life's most important question? Is it not, "To be or not to be?"

9. Irvin Yalom: What do you really want?

Glossary

Absurdity: Simply, the fact that life has no meaning. In addition, for Camus, it is the world's indifference to our rational expectations of justice, satisfaction, and happiness.

Alienation: For Yalom, it refers to the feeling of separation from other people, the world around us, and even ourselves. He also refers to *alienation* as *ultimate aloneness*.

Antinatalism: Associated with David Benatar, it is the belief that bringing children into the world is an immoral act, given the difficulty and pain of life. Further, since it is impossible for children to have a choice in their own existence, it is a violation of their free will.

Anxiety: For Kierkegaard, it is the natural state of human beings because we can imagine the future and contemplate choices without a certain knowledge of the outcome of our choices.

Authenticity: The degree to which we live independently of social pressures to depart from our true character and internalized sense of how we should live.

Bad Faith: Sartre's term for any form of self-deception, especially when we deceive ourselves by looking to others to define us or defining ourselves by our intentions rather than the effects of our actions.

Being-Towards-Death: For Heidegger, as well as Yalom and Frankl, the importance of living with a continual awareness of our mortality.

Cogito ergo sum: Translated as, "I think, therefore, I am." Posited by Rene Descartes as the one thing of which we can be certain.

Das Man: Heidegger's term for the inauthentic self, the self constructed by our experience with other people. Sartre communicated the same idea with his well-known quotation, "Hell is other people" and the concept "bad faith."

Dasein: Heidegger's conception of "the being through whom being comes into question." Dasein literally means "being there," communicating Heidegger's insistence that human beings cannot be understood apart from their environment, which is the world. It is the environment that provides the stimuli for perceptions.

Death: For Yalom, it is the inevitable event we avoid thinking about because of the anxiety it generates. For Heidegger, death is *indefinite* and *non-relational*. It is *indefinite* because, with few exceptions, we do not know how and when we will die. It is *non-relational* because we cannot experience it through the death of someone else.

eligo: Translated as, "I choose." Posited by Jaspers as the unique human capacity to make decisions and act on them. *Eligo* goes beyond "thinking" to "choosing" and "acting."

Empiricism: For Jaspers, one of the three paths to knowledge, also referred to as the scientific method of discovery and description by experimentation. He emphasized this method is limited in the knowledge it can provide.

Eternal Recurrence: Nietzsche's thought experiment by which he invites us to examine our life by asking if we would like to relive it, in every detail, an infinite number of times in eternity. The implication of this question is if we would not like an *eternal recurrence* of our life, what do we need to do to make *eternal recurrence* a pleasing thought?

Ethical Relativism: The philosophical position that there exists no objective standard for "right" and "wrong" behavior. Therefore, "right" and "wrong" are subjectively determined by individuals, communities or situations.

Existentialism: The philosophical movement derived from and emphasizing free will and personal responsibility. Its earliest expression as a distinct school of thought are the nineteenth century writings of Kierkegaard and Nietzsche. Prominent twentieth century existential voices are those of Heidegger, Sartre, and Camus.

Existential Isolation: For Yalom, the alienation we feel from ourselves, others, and the world around us. This distancing results from our imperfect knowledge of ourselves, others, and the world.

Facticity: Sartre's term for the unchangeable, brute facts that characterize us, such as our height, parents, date of birth, hometown, etc.

Forlornness: The feeling that comes upon us when we realize no one can help us make sense of our existence. Like a prisoner of war held in solitary confinement, we are on own to determine what we need to do if our existence is to have meaning.

Individuality: There is no philosophy, religion, science or any other system of thought that can provide us with the meaning of life. There is no "suit off the rack;" there is no "one-size-fits-all." All suits are "tailor made" by the wearer.

Intuitionalism: For Jaspers, one of the three paths to knowledge. Knowledge that has not been acquired by scientific evidence or reason but is nevertheless embraced as true is the product of intuition. Blaise Pascal's well-known statement characterizes intuitionalism: "The heart has its reasons that reason cannot comprehend."

Leap-to-Faith: Kierkegaard's concept of action taken in the absence of knowledge from reason or science. Similar to intuitionalism, a leap-to-faith occurs when something intangible and unprovable is considered an adequate motivation for action. Kierkegaard offered the biblical patriarch Abraham as a paradigm of a *leap-to-faith*.

Ockham's Razor: Also known as the *principle of parsimony*, it teaches that explanations should be as uncomplicated as possible. Its Latin expression is, *Entia non sunt multiplicanda praeter necessitatem*. Translated into English, it reads, "Entities should not be multiplied beyond necessity."

Passionate Engagement: Not everyone has the same interests. One of life's challenges is to discover the activities that truly matter to us and pursue them. This discovery is essential to an authentic life. For Frankl, virtually everyday, life provides innumerable opportunities for personally meaningful activity.

Phenomenology: The philosophical school of thought that provided a foundation for existentialism. It is the study of *how* we experience our existence. In other words, in phenomenology *perception* is more important than *reality* because actions are driven by what we perceive rather than objective reality even if there is such a thing as objective reality.

Rationalism: For Jaspers, one of the three paths to knowledge, also referred to as reason. For Kierkegaard, it is limited in its ability to locate answers in certain situations, therefore sometimes leaving a leap-to-faith as the basis for action.

Rejection of Meaning-Giving-Narratives: There is no story from literature, fiction or nonfiction, that can provide us with the purpose of our life. The French essayist and playwright Gabriel Marcel (1889-1973) inquired into the meaning of life by arousing the dramatic imagination. But he even agreed with Camus that we bear the weight of our own existence.

Responsibility: The fundamental existential belief that we create our identity and life situations by our actions. Further, each of us is solely accountable for the consequences that emanate from our behavior.

Sisyphus: The mythological King of Ephyra who was condemned by the gods to an eternity of rolling a boulder up a hill only to have it roll down the hill each time it reached the top. Camus used Sisyphus to describe the meaningless life of the workingman who labors unaware of his plight.

Suicide: For Camus, the one truly philosophical problem is whether life is worth living.

Thrownness: For Heidegger, it describes our entrance into life. Without our permission we are cast into a hostile, unsympathetic world and challenged to make sense of our existence and live a personally meaningful life.

Tragic Optimism: Frankl's belief that life's three unavoidable tragedies (pain, guilt, and death) can be used to our advantage if we so decide and act to make the most of them.

Transcendence: Sartre's term for the human capacity to choose to go beyond the unchangeable, brute facts that characterize us.

Ubermensch: Variously translated as "the superman" or "the overman," it is Nietzsche's concept of a fully developed human being who is more than a human being. The *Ubermensch* is not given to superstition (especially religion) and establishes his own morality rather than blindly following society's code of conduct.

Will to Meaning: For Frankl it is the fundamental human drive to live a life that is purposeful.

Will to Power: For Nietzche, it is the fundamental human drive to have control over ourselves and our environment.

References

Preface

Pojman, L. (1991). *Introduction to philosophy: Classical and contemporary readings.* Belmont, CA: Wadsworth Publishing.

Introduction

Camus, A. (2014). Recovered from Thinkexist.com website on 07/03/2014.

Livgren, K. (1977). "Dust in the wind." Album: "Point of no return." Label: Kirschner.

Lonergan, K. (2011). "Margaret." Fox Searchlight Pictures.

Jobs, S. (2005). Recovered from the 06/15/2005 news.stanford.edu website on 07/04/2014

Jung, C. (2014). Recovered from BrainyQuote website on 07/03/2014.

Peck, S. (1983). *People of the lie: The hope for healing human evil.* New York: Simon and Schuster.

Sartre, J.P. (1957). *Existentialism and human emotions.* New York: Citadel Press. Kensington Publishing Group.

Solomon, R. (2000). *No excuses: Existentialism and the meaning of life.* Chantilly, VA; The Teaching Company.

Szasz, T. (1973). *The second sin.* Garden City, NY: Anchor Press. Doubleday and Company.

I. Soren Kierkegaard

Bonhoeffer, D. (1995). *The cost of discipleship.* New York: Touchstone Press.

Cogswell, D. (2008). *Existentialism for beginners.* Hanover, NH: Steerforth Press.

Eliot, T.S. (1915). "The love song of J. Alfred Prufrock." *Poetry.* London, UK: The Egoist, Ltd.

Jobs, S. (2005). Recovered from the 06/15/2005 news.stanford.-edu/news website on 07/04/2014.

Kierkegaard, S. (2014). Recovered from Quotes of Kierkegaard. website on 07/03/2014.

Kinsella, W. (1982). *Shoeless Joe.* Boston, MA: Houghton Mifflin.

Sorkin, A. (1989). "A Few Good Men." Castle Rock Entertainment.

II. Friedrich Nietzsche

Craig, W. (2008). *Reasonable faith: Christian theology and apologetics.* Wheaton, IL: Crossway Books.

Darrow, C. (2014). Recovered from American Experience/Monkey Trial/People and Events website on 07/04/2014.

Dostoevsky, F. (2014). Although this quotation has frequently been attributed to Fyodor Dostoevsky as part of *The Brothers Karamazov* it is nowhere to be found in this work. However, the idea conveyed by this quotation is present in the book. The closest quotation in the book is: "If there is no immortality, then all things are permitted" (Dostoevsky, F. *The brothers Karamazov.* translated C. Garnett. New York: Signet Classics. 1957. book II, chapter 6; book V, chapter 4; book XI, chapter 8.

Nietzsche, F. (2014). Recovered from Thinkexist.com website on 07/04/2014.

_____. (1966). *Beyond good and evil.* Walter Kaufmann, translator. New York: Random House.

_____. (1974). *The gay science.* Walter Kaufmann, translator. New York: Vintage Books.

_____. (1976). *Thus spake Zarathustra: A book for all or none.* Walter Kaufmann, translator. New York: Random House.

Yalom, I. (2008). *Staring at the sun: Overcoming the terror of death.* San Francisco, CA: Jossey Bass.

III. Karl Jaspers

Jaspers, K. (2014). Recovered from Thinkexist.com website on 07/04/2014.

Pascal, B. (20141). Recovered from Thinkexist.com website on 07/04/2014.

_____. (1971). *Philosophy of existence*. Richard Grabau, translator. Philadelphia, PA: University of Pennsylvania Press.

Wallace, D. (2009). *This is water: Some thoughts delivered on a significant occasion, about living a compassionate life*. New York: Little Brown and Company.

IV. Martin Heidegger

Benatar, D. (2006). *Better never to have been: The harm of coming into existence*. Oxford, UK: Oxford University Press.

Critchley, S. (2009). "Being and Time; Part 6" *The Guardian*. 07/13/200

Frankl, V. (1959). *Man's search for meaning*. New York: Washington Square Press.

Heidegger, M. (1962). *Being and time*. New York: Harper and Row.

Menand, L. (2014). "The Prisoner of Stress." *The New Yorker*. 01/27/2014.

Morrison, J. (1971). "Riders on the Storm." Recovered from AZLyrics.com on 07/06/2014.

Trueblood, D. (1951). *The life we prize*. New York: Harper and Row.

Young, J. (1997). *Heidegger, philosophy, naziism*. Cambridge, UK: Cambridge University Press.

V. Viktor Frankl

Cronkite, K. (1994). *On the edge of darkness: Conversations about conquering depression.* New York: Doubleday Publishing Company.

Frankl, V. (1959). *Man's search for meaning.* New York: Washington Square Press.

_____ . (1964). *The will to meaning: Foundations and applications of logotherapy.* New York: Penguin Group.

_____ . (2014). Recovered from <u>Thinkexist.com</u> on 07/06/2014.

Malikow, M. (2014). *It's not too late: Making the most of the rest of your life.* Chipley, FL: Theocentric Publishing.

VI. Jean-Paul Sartre

Frost, R. (1911). Although this definition has been attributed to others, including Mark Twain, it was   spoken by Frost in a conversation with Sidney Cox. Recovered from the <u>Robert Frost Society</u> website on 07/07/2014.

Katen, T. (1973). *Doing philosophy.* Englewood Cliffs, NJ: Prentice Hall.

Sartre, J. (1957). *Existentialism and human emotions.* New York: Kensington Publishing Corp.

_____ . (2007). Recovered from <u>Thinkexist.com</u> on 07/07/2014.

_____ . (1947). *The flies.* New York: Alfred A. Knopf, Inc.

_____ .(2014). Recovered from <u>Thinkexist.com</u> website on 07/04/2014.

Wartenberg, T. (2008). *Existentialism*. Oxford, UK: One world Publications.

Woodward, K. (2010). "The most famous thing Jean-Paul Sartre never said." Followers: Rick on Theatre. 07/09/2010.

VII. Simone de Beauvoir

Cogswell, D. (2008). *Existentialism for beginners*. Hanover, NH: Steerforth Press.

de Beauvoir, S. (1954). *The ethics of ambiguity*. Seacucus, NJ: Citadel Press.

Moore, C. (2010). Recovered from Philosophy Now: A Magazine of Ideas website. May/June 2010 on 07/07/2014.

VIII. Albert Camus

Blackburn, V. (2011). "The Challenge of the Unbeliever." Scottish Journal of Theology, 64, 313-326. 08/2011.

Camus, A. (1955*). The myth of Sisyphus and other essays*. New York: Alfred A. Knopf, Inc.

de Beauvoir, S. (2014). Recovered from Thinkexist.com on 07/07/2014.

Livingston, G. (2004) *To soon old, too late smart: Thirty true things you need to know*. New York: Marlow and Company.

Wartenberg, T. (2008). *Existentialism*. Oxford, UK: One world Publications.

Whitman, W. (1900). "O Me! O Life!" *Leaves of Grass*. Recovered from Bartleby.com website on 07/07/2014.

Yeats, W, (2014). Recovered from Thinkexist.com on 07/07/2014.

IX. Irvin Yalom

Chance, S. (1992). *Stronger than death: When suicide touches your life - a mother's story*. NewYork: W.W. Norton.

Frankl, V. (1964). *The will to meaning: Foundations and applications of logotherapy*. New York: Penguin Group.

Powell, J. (1969). *Why am i afraid to tell you who i am: Insights into personal growth*. Allen, TX: Thomas More.

Wolfe, T. (1929). *Look homeward angel*. New York: Scribner.

Yalom, I. (1980). *Existential psychotherapy*. New York: Basic Books, Inc., Publishers.

_____ . (1989). *Love's executioner and other tales of psychotherapy*. New York: Basic Books, Inc., Publishers.

_____ . (2008). *Staring at the sun: Overcoming the terror of death*. San Francisco, CA: Jossey-Bass.

_____ . (1992). *When Nietzsche wept*. New York: HarperCollins Publishers.

www.ingramcontent.com/pod-product-compliance
Lightning Source LLC
Chambersburg PA
CBHW070906280326
41934CB00008B/1611